THE CONSPIRACY COLORING BOOK

FOR ADULTS ONLY

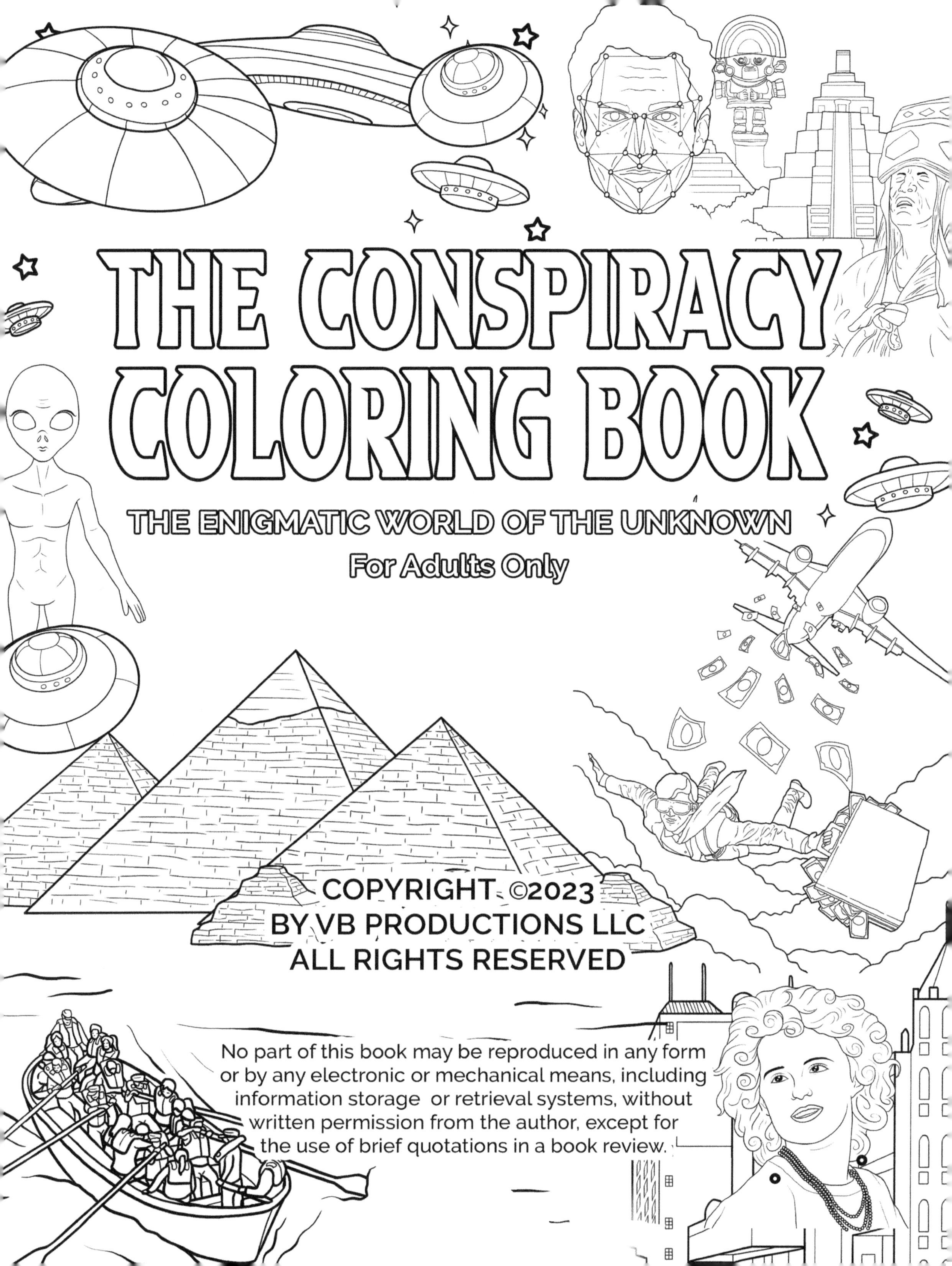

THE CONSPIRACY COLORING BOOK

THE ENIGMATIC WORLD OF THE UNKNOWN

For Adults Only

STOP
DO NOT ENTER
RESTRICTED AREA
DO NOT ENTER
EXTRATERRESTRIAL HIGHWAY
AREA 51

THE ILLUMINATI

BERMUDA TRIANGLE

THE EGYPTIAN PYRAMIDS

THE LOCH NESS MONSTER

STONEHENGE

BIGFOOT

WELCOME TO
ROSWELL

LOST CITY
OF ATLANTIS

JACK THE RIPPER

HOLLYWOOD
BLACK DAHLIA

ALIEN CROP CIRCLES

STARGATE PORTALS

WANTED
ZODIAC KILLER

THE JFK
ASSASSINATION

NAZCA LINES

EL DORADO

D.B. COOPER

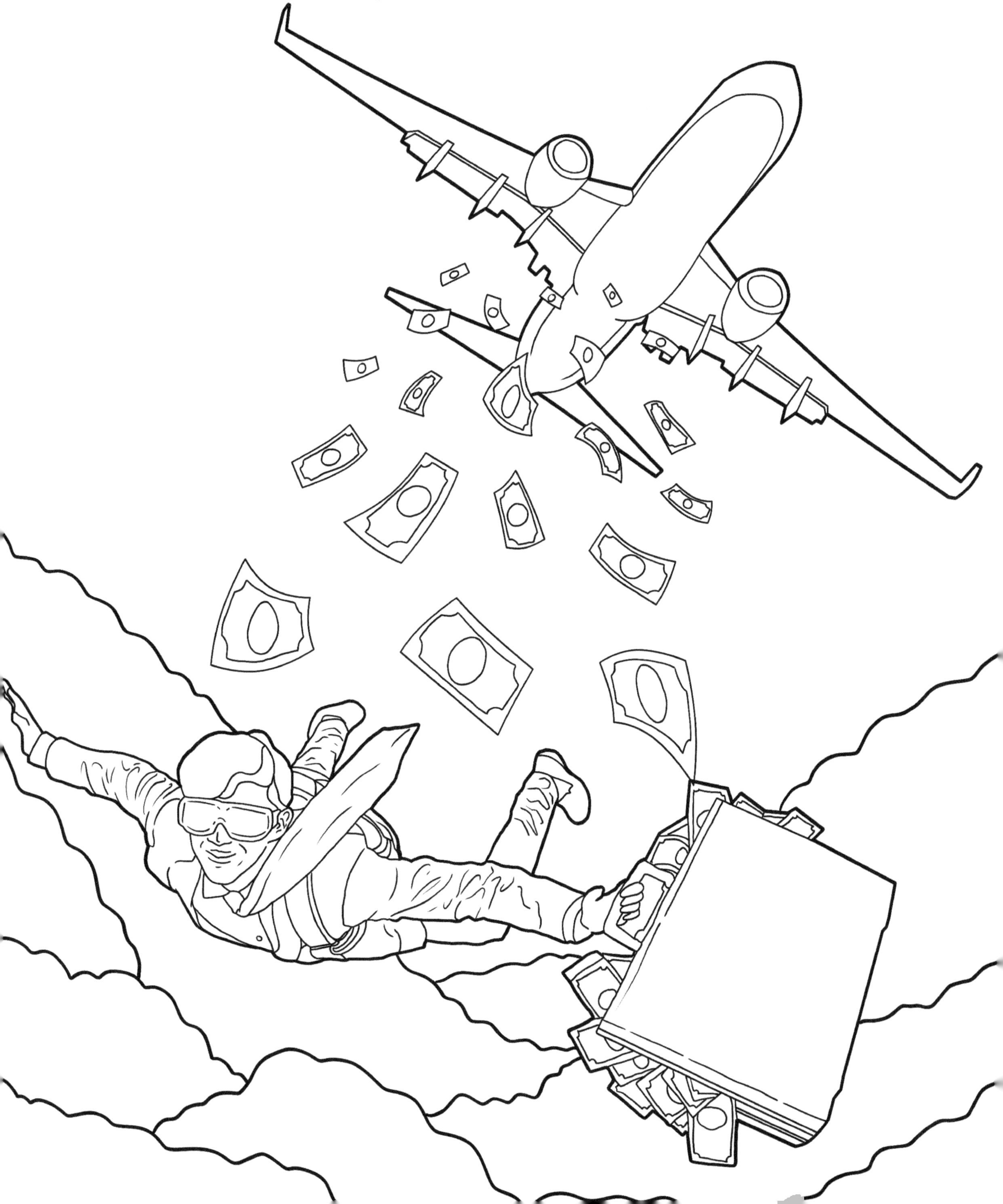

MISSING
TEAMSTERS UNION
THE DISAPPEARANCE OF JIMMY HOFFA

THE LOST
AMBER ROOM

CLEOPATRA'S TOMB

TOP SECRET
BIG BROTHER

THE HOLY GRAIL

GEORGIA GUIDESTONES

SINKING OF THE TITANIC

www.ingramcontent.com/pod-product-compliance
Lightning Source LLC
LaVergne TN
LVHW072129060526
838201LV00071B/4998
* 9 7 9 8 8 6 9 0 8 5 9 3 1 *